Cover

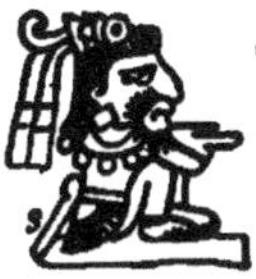

# THE CLIFF-DWELLERS

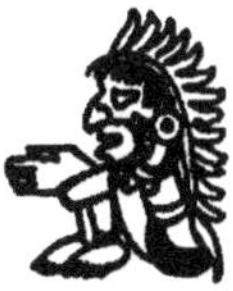

An Account of their Organization, the Dedication and Opening of their Quarters, Constitution and By-Laws, Officers, Committees, and List of Members

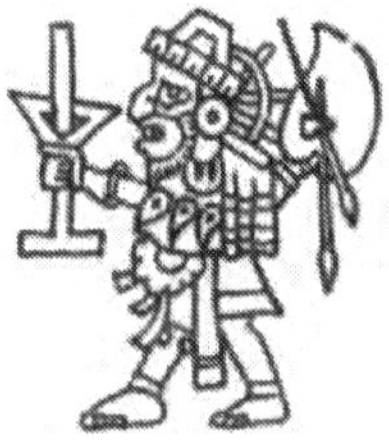

CHICAGO
168 MICHIGAN AVENUE
MCMX

From the
Presidents Office

## CONTENTS.

| | |
|---|---|
| Short History of the Genesis of the Club | p. 5 |
| Story of the Fire-Lighting Ceremony | p. 11 |
| Address | p. 23 |
| Letters of Greeting | p. 43 |
| Officers, Council and Committees of the Club | p. 54 |
| Constitution and By-Laws | p. 59 |
| Members | p. 71 |

## A SHORT HISTORY OF THE GENESIS OF THE CLUB

EARLY in June, 1907, Mr. Hamlin Garland, after consultation with Messrs. Ralph Clarkson, Lorado Taft, Allen B. Pond, and one or two other friends, sent out a letter to a list of men representing the various arts, asking for an expression of opinion with regard to the desirability of a club which should be to the city of Chicago something of what the Players and the Century Association are to the city of New York, and inviting those who cared to assist in the formation of such a club to meet him at the City Club for luncheon.

On June 12th the following men came together: Chas. F. Browne, Ralph Clarkson, Clarence Dickinson, Hamlin Garland, Wallace Heckman, Chas. L. Hutchinson, A. B. Pond, I. K. Pond, A. A. Michelson, Robt. Milliken, Rollin B. Salisbury, Herbert S. Stone and

Lorado Taft. Mr. Garland presided, presenting a general idea of the club and asked for suggestions. It was agreed that the gathering of names for a Committee on Organization was the first work to be done and Mr. Garland read the following sketch of a letter to be sent out to a still larger list of names. This letter was to be signed by the members who had already given their consent to serve on such a committee. The letter read as follows:

"DEAR SIR:—The above named committee invite you to assist in the formation of a club, to be known as the Midland Arts Club of America. There are in Chicago many clubs, each with a special function, civil or political, but there is no association which unites all the literary and artistic forces as this club would do. Broadly speaking, this club will bring together men of artistic and literary tastes who are now widely scattered among the various social and business organizations of Chicago, and unite them with the artists, writers, architects and musicians of the city in a club whose purposes are distinctly and primarily aesthetic. The dues are to be kept so low that no young artist or writer will find them a burden. Club rooms will be established at some very central point, and a noon-day round-table will be a feature of the club life.

"The membership is to be composed of—

"First; men concerned with some form of creative art; that is to say, painters, sculptors, novelists, poets, musicians, architects, historians, illustrators and those who make handicraft and art.

"Second; distinguished men in other professions who are patrons of art or sympathetic with the fundamental purposes of the club.

"The Committee of Organization already contains distinguished members of the Union League, the City Club, the Chicago Club, the Chicago Society of Artists, the Architectural Club, the Little Room, the Literary Club, the Quadrangle Club and the Amateur Musical Club.

"No such synthesis of the aesthetic forces of western life has hitherto been attempted, but we believe the time has come when it can be made. We invite you to signify your willingness to accept membership on this committee, believing that you will find the proposed club of immediate interest and of growing importance."

The members present endorsed this letter as one proper to be sent out and it was moved and seconded that Mr. Garland be made chairman of the committee and that he be empowered to proceed in the work of securing representative men to serve on this committee. The meeting then adjourned, to meet one week later.

At the second meeting, the tentative name, The Midland Arts, was debated. Mr. Garland's report was as follows:

"Your committee has to report the most gratifying success in enlarging the membership of the Committee of Organization. Not a single refusal has come in, and not one of all those to whom the purposes of the club have been explained has failed of enthusiastic response. Your chairman has had the most valuable aid from Frederick Stock and Clarence Dickinson. The musical side of the committee is sure to be well filled and of representative character. Mr. Clarkson, Mr. Taft, Mr. Browne and Mr. Irving Pond have been of great service in building up the list of painters, sculptors and architects; and Mr. A. B. Pond and Mr. Charles L. Hutchinson have been of equal service in bringing together representative business men of aesthetic tastes."

There were present and voting at this meeting Chas. F. Browne, Ralph Clarkson, Lorado

Taft, A. B. Pond, I. K. Pond, Hugh Garden, Howard Shaw, Chas. D. Norton, Alfred H. Granger, Jens Jensen, Robt. Herrick, Robt. M. Lovett, Roswell Field, A. A. Michelson, Robt. Milliken and Dwight H. Perkins.

On motion, Mr. Garland as Chairman was empowered to appoint an Executive Committee of nine members of the Committee of Organization, and he selected the following men: Chas. L. Hutchinson, Frederick C. Bartlett, Lorado Taft, Clarence Dickinson, Howard Shaw, Alfred H. Granger, I. K. Pond, Ralph Clarkson and Hobart C. Chatfield-Taylor. The sentiment of all present was that the time had come for the successful founding of such a club.

For several successive Saturdays the committee met at luncheon at the City Club and entered upon the work of choosing a name and forming a constitution. Mr. A. B. Pond was elected temporary secretary and during the entire summer and early fall the committee struggled over the problem of securing quarters within The Loop, and indeed this continued to be a very grave problem until at last the Orchestra Hall Association consented to permit the club, which had finally adopted the name, "The Cliff Dwellers," to build upon its roof.

The formal organization of the club was made in January, 1908, when members of the Committee of Organization and prospective members of the club, to the number of 95, gathered in the studio of Ralph Clarkson. Mr. Garland, as chairman of the committee, called the meeting to order and asked Harry Pratt Judson, of the University of Chicago, to preside. Mr. Wallace Heckman was nominated and elected temporary secretary. Mr. Garland then read his report, reciting what had been done and presented a constitution, together with the name, "The Cliff Dwellers." This report was accepted almost unanimously and the formal organization of the club was complete.

During the year that followed, the most important committee of the club was the building committee, composed of Chas. L. Hutchinson, Howard Shaw, I. K. Pond, Arthur T. Aldis and Alfred Granger, but it was not until January 6th of 1908 that the club was able to take possession of its "Khiva" on the top of Orchestra Hall. The opening of the club room was made notable by a fire-lighting program, of which the following report, taken from "The Bookman" of New York City, is a fairly accurate account:

A distinguished recent addition to Literary Clubland is the Cliff Dwellers' Club of Chicago, which was opened with a housewarming last month. In modeling the Cliff Dwellers the organizers had in mind three clubs, the Century and the Players of New York and the Bohemian of San Francisco, aiming to take something from the spirit or the constitution of each of these corporations. The opening ceremonies were exceedingly elaborate. Greetings were sent from the Tavern Club of Boston, the Bohemian Club of San Francisco, the Franklin Inn Club of Philadelphia, the Cosmos Club of Washington, and the Century, Authors, Players and Lambs of New York.

### Part I. Primitive.

The first part of the programme, called "Traditional," was a pageant symbolizing the position of the club with regard to all America, emphasizing its central location. The lines for this ceremony by Thomas W. Stevens were recited by Donald Robertson, master of the pageant. After the members had been massed against the east wall and under the dim light from two blue electric bulbs the master in these words evoked the Shades:

> Not with one voice we speak, nor with one torch
> This solemn hour illuminate: our hearths
> New-built and virgin to the cheer of fire,
> Our home walls filleting a city's brow,
> And all our light and glow and pulse of hope
> Wait here their sign, their wakening into life.
> Now lest we hold too close this running year,
> Its untraditioned splendor—gold and steel,
> And the triumphant march of toiling men,
> We call the dwellers of the ancient dusk,
> Call to the finders of the golden way,
> And the stern spirits, furrowing wintry deeps,
> Who hither fled from alien tyrannies.
> No starry pageant of immortal shapes,
> Nor ancestry of death begotten kings,
> But men—simple and strong and valiant men,
> Who did their work in past, fulfilling here
> Their simple, undivided destinies.

In response to this evocation the Cliff Dwellers sang from below the words of a song written by Hamlin Garland, and set to music by Olaf Anderson, beginning with the humming refrain, "From Si-pa-pu We Come, We Come," as if in answer to the call of the Master of the pageant. As they entered, the Master's voice was again heard in these lines:

Behold the dwellers of the Nether Cliffs!
Up from their dreary, rock-bound citadels,
Threading the ledges worn by patient feet
Of generations that had died ere Troy
Went down in thunder echoing into song.
Ghosts from the dim gray morn of time, we greet you:
For our high name, and for this meagre spark,
Hard-won from whirling wood and stricken flint,
We give you thanks.

Four plains Indians then appeared, one of them bearing a peace pipe, and to them the Master gravely spoke:

And you, grave warriors,
Stubbornly yielding what you could not rule,
We welcome you as well. For in this hall
Shall dwell no strife; from you the Calumet,
The peace-pipe, and the azure clouds that rise
Into the still air when the songs are mute.

At this moment the Spanish explorers approached and stood in silence while the Master addressed them:

Spaniards, who tramp the desert grim in steel,
We take of you the inexorable flame
That beckoned you across the mystery,
And made the dim horizon open trails
To your undaunted and adventurous march.

A group of French missionaries glided forward, and the Master acknowledged their services to the West:

> Fathers, who from the pined and drifted north
> Came down along the still, uncharted ways,
> Bearing the cross of an engendering faith—
> You bring us a white light of ecstasy,
> A spirit that endures through bleaker years,
> A faith that shall not break nor burn away
> In all the dust and fever of our toil—
> Our "Little Fathers of the Wilderness."

In vivid contrast to these missionaries came the cavaliers of Virginia, booted and plumed.

> Men of Virginia, blades of Raleigh's choice,
> We greet you for the flowering courtesy,
> The gentleness that met ungentle days
> And was not stained; we take of you the torch
> Of golden hospitalities gone by,
> And on this hearth we lay its generous fire.

Next came the Puritans, in gray cloaks and peaked hats.

> But not alone to gentler airs and times,
> Not mirth alone, nor music, nor delight,
> Shall we be dedicate; for in our blood
> The stern heroical and Pilgrim strain,
> The chanting of old hymns, the love of toil,
> The deeper love of freedom under law,
> (Gaunt virtues of the Puritans) abide.

Types of pioneers, soldiers of the Revolution and other American and later settlers, entered together.

> So all the strong forerunners of our race,
> The finders of the way, the nation-makers,
> Bring brands alight, and in this symbol fling
> Upon our fire the glamour of their deeds,
> About our hearth their history; the past
> Speaks in these gathered sparks: no weary word,

No drowsy song of legend or of spell,
But the keen triumph of the harvest tide.

The procession passed before the hearth, and each character threw into it his torch in token of his contribution to this central flame of hospitality. And as they passed, the Master said this final word of blessing:

So be of good cheer, and hope, and fellowship,
Clear fortune to our unretreating star,
And prosperous days and mighty dreams fulfilled,
The issues of this hour. And to our house
Stability and honor through the years,
And to this hearth the lasting grace of life.

Led by the primitives, the procession moved in silence before the hearth and in shadowy file vanished back to "Si-pa-pu," the Cliff Dweller underworld singing these words:

We must away,
Vanishing below
To Si-pa-pu, to Si-pa-pu.

As the voices died away, the Master of the pageant kindled the fire and the Club quartet, Mr. Marion Green, Mr. John B. Miller, Mr. George Hamlin and Dr. Wm. Williams, directed by Clarence Dickinson, sang the Club hymn, written by Wallace Rice and set to music by Frederick Stock.

### Part II. Modern.

Hamlin Garland, the president of the club, taking from Mr. Robertson (the Master of the pageant) the Calumet, led the way to the north hearth in the dining-room, and there, while the members remained standing, Mr. Garland laid the pipe upon the mantel. He then read the following lines, anouncing the gift of driftwood by the Tavern Club of Boston:

From the gray Atlantic, from their pent-in home-place,
  From the ancient hub and central fount of verse,
The Taverners of Boston, a genial club and antic,
  Have sent paternal greetings, nothing worse.
Here, beside our hearth, behold, a bar'l of driftwood,
  Caught from the foaming breakers of Cape Ann.
Hinting in this, the story of the whaler,
  Who fears no mood of ocean or of man.

For us, the timid sons of peaceful plain and prairie,
  Our cousins of the ledge and battering wave,
Have set before our eyes the rainbow flames upleaping
  To fill our hearts with worship of the brave.
Grateful to all who sailed the seas before us,
  Glad to claim a kinship with New England's lofty names,
Ancestral in our turn, we raise this inland temple
  And hopefully confront the challenge of your flames.

Here the president of the Cliff Dwellers read the following lines by Mark A. De Wolfe Howe, of the Tavern Club, and cast upon the fire a bit of the briny, copper-stained wood:

## WITH DRIFTWOOD TO THE CLIFF-DWELLERS.

Drifted from leagues of sunlit waves,
 Forth from the ancient east,
Your kindling care this token craves
 That fain would light your feast.

And when upon your hearth its flame
 Flings the pent banner out,
Gleams of the sunrise whence it came
 Shall flash your halls about.

The altar-fires of all the arts
 Shall glow on hearth-stones new;
The life that fellowship imparts—
 Long may it quicken you!

So let the fiery letters spell
 A greeting warm and free
To you in beetling Cliffs who Dwell,
 From a Tavern by the sea.
—M. A. DeWolfe Howe.
Tavern Club, Boston, January 4, 1909.

The president of the club then announced in the following lines a similar gift of driftwood from the Bohemian Club of San Francisco:

From the golden gate, from far Pacific breakers,
 From the land of Spanish legend, gold and wine,
Our brothers of Bohemia have sent us, with their blessing,
 A rock-worn ship's beam, rescued from the brine—
Dug from the beach whose shining, fabled rivers
 Allured our fathers westward across the desert sand,
Evoking here tonight the Shades of Clark and Lewis
 And the Argonauts of fifty—that bearded iron band.

California, whose very name is music,
 We greet your words of bounty with gratitude and glee;

To our bare hearth your generous hands have given
  The romance of the galleon, the glamour of the sea.
Beyond Harte's Poker Flat and Joaquin's high Sierras,
  Past John Muir's parks and Markham's cedars tall,
We send an answering cry of middle-western greeting
  And bid you share the plenty of our hall.

Mr. Garland then read "The Cliff Dwellers," by George Sterling, of the Bohemian Club:

### "THE CLIFF-DWELLERS."

As men of old from beast or human foe
  Sought them a stony lair,
So all today seek ever, high and low,
  Refuge from prowling Care.

The hollowed cliff far up its covert gave,
  By notched and giddy path,
Where walled and imminent the age-worn cave
  Mocked at the outer wrath.

Today our foe is subtler, and in vain
  The fortalice of old:
He comes with whispered grief and hidden pain—
  Unseen, or mailed in gold.

And respite for a little time, at best,
  In that long war we find—
A breathing-space to give the heart its rest,
  Its silence to the mind.

A shelter high amid the parceled walls
  That house our urgent race,
Where men in brotherhood find equal halls
  And strifeless resting-place.

Where Bacchic poppies on the fretted nerve
  Their languors cast awhile,
And Art, the angel pitiless we serve,
  Stands with atoning smile.

>Since in your center of enduring war
>  A refuge high you gain,
>Take, too, our greeting from a distant shore,
>  Our tribute from its main.
>
>Forget awhile that mortals, one by one,
>  At last shall driftwood be,
>Cast on the beaches of oblivion
>  By life's rejecting sea.
>
>Bright be the beacon of your firstling fire,
>  A flame that cannot cease,
>To Joy a shrine, to Care an endless pyre,
>  To men a pledge of peace.
>              —GEORGE STERLING.

Mr. Garland alluded to the Players' Club of New York in these lines:

>At the still center of Manhattan's frenzy,
>On a small plot which fronts upon a tree,
>Stands the Players' house, by Edwin Booth provided.
>To be the central fane of modern minstrelsy.
>No other of our clubs exceeds it in tradition,
>Just as no other player o'ertops its founder's fame,
>Taught by his words, by his example guided,
>We seek the Players' blessing on our name.

Mr. Otis Skinner, officially delegated to speak for the Players, read their formal greeting, engrossed upon a card, and added a few words of his own in explanation of the purposes of the Players and in greeting to the Cliff-Dwellers, wishing them a long and merry life.

The National Institute through its counsel Wm. M. Sloane (president), Robert Underwood Johnson (secretary), sent its well wishes.

In addition to the official greetings on the part of similar organizations, Mr. Garland read letters from President Roosevelt, Colonel Thomas Wentworth Higginson and Edward Everett Hale, of Boston; William Dean Howells, of New York; Joaquin Miller, of Oakland, California; Charles F. Lummis, of Los Angeles, California; Edwin Markham, of Oregon; James Whitcomb Riley, of Indianapolis; S. Weir Mitchell, of Philadelphia, and Professor Brander Matthews, of Columbia University. Professor Matthews contributed a poem:

ON THE HEIGHTS<br>
A Greeting to the Cliff-Dwellers.

Hail! Ye men of lofty station
Looking down upon the nation,
From your eyrie of elation
    And relief;
Hail! Ye dwellers in a far land,
On a peak and up near starland,
With your hamlin-culture's garland
    For a chief!

All the milliners and drapers,
Advertising in the papers,
Cannot fill the tall skyscrapers
    To the top;
And there's room, somewhere above them
For the arts, and those that love them,
Where the crowd can't crush and shove them
    Till they drop.

It was Goethe who has said it,
And it's greatly to his credit;
(In your memory now imbed it
    Once for all,
With no further dilly dally).
"There is peace above the valley,"
Where the setting sun-rays rally
    Ere they fall.

There is peace and there is pleasure
Better far than buried treasure
For the men who earn their leisure
    Shirking not;
There is peace and there is laughter,
Rising warmly to the rafter,
There is scorn for crook and grafter
    Burning hot.

May your culture go on humming!
May your notions keep on coming!
May your scribbling and your strumming
    Both excel!
May your shadow ne'er diminish!
May your atmosphere get thinnish!
May you fight fate to a finish!
    Fare you well.

Charles F. Lummis contributed four lines:

### THE CLIFF-DWELLERS

I, too, am red with the sun that browned them—
  To know their hearts you must learn their tan—
Brown, but our younger selves, I found them,
  For the man is a child—and the child is man.

Augustus Thomas, Shepherd of the Lambs, in his official communication, said:

The Lambs, by nature led to pastures and rich lowlands, have long felt that the loftier, sterile and more exposed jags were insufficiently grazed. There is a significance in your name that promises improvement in this regard. We prophesy no biblical separation of the flock, but hope, on the contrary, that the topographical and geological placements may permit a marginal blending.

Mr. Gilder, speaking for the Century Association, wrote:

As chairman of the Committee on Literature of the Century Association, I am authorized to extend to the Cliff-Dwellers most hearty fraternal greetings from the association in New York which was so long ago established with like spirit and intent. From the height of our own long and happy history, we wish you a fortunate beginning and an everlasting continuing in your dwelling on the cliffs.

Introducing the Franklin Inn Club poem, Mr. Garland again dropped into rhyme:

From staid Philadelphia, from the home of old-time
    Quaker,
From the Franklin Inn, a meeting house of friends,
Comes this fair scroll, so quaint and curt and seemly,
A writ of admonition where wit with humour blends.

May their plain speech and brotherly intending
The closer knit our little band of men,
Well may we take from Pennsylvania manners
The tolerance of Franklin, the courtesy of Penn.

The poem of the Franklin Inn Club was engraved upon a card by its author, Felix N. Gerson:

    We place gray hairs upon our youth,
      And other antique mummery,
    That you may think, in very truth,
      'Tis Franklin's self whom here you see—

    For with a pointed line or two
      We limn a visage old and wise,

>     And stalk among your merry crew
>         With serious goggles on our eyes.
>
>     So that, Cliff-Dwellers of the West,
>         In these gray greetings that we send,
>     Beneath the Quaker's coat and vest
>         You'll find the heart-beats of a "Friend"—
>     And as we clasp you by the hand,
>         Just take a little nearer view,
>     And you will recognize our brand—
>         We're jolly youngsters just like you!

The main addresses of the evening were delivered by Mr. Robert Herrick, representing literature; Mr. Charles L. Hutchinson, representing the lay membership, and Mr. Lorado Taft, who spoke for painting and sculpture.

## OUR PREDECESSORS.
### ADDRESS BY ROBERT HERRICK.

WHEN our kindly presiding officer asked me to speak on this occasion, I demurred on the ground that whatever I might have to say would be serious, and that my dull remarks might tend to cast a shade of solemnity on what should be above all else a joyous festival. "Be as serious as you like!" was his cheerful reply. Apparently he is optimist enough to believe that the Cliff Dwellers can stand any sober reflections of mine, and with his encouragement I intend, fellow members of the Cliff Dwellers, to speak for a few minutes of serious things in an earnest mood.

The topic suggested to me—as a transplanted New Englander—was "Our Predecessors." But I, too, in my way, am an optimist, and cannot confine myself exclusively to the dead, to recounting the past. I must have my fling at Prophecy. . . . . Our Predecessors—I take it that we mean by that the East. For, as surely as the call of material ambition for our race has been westward, the call of the spirit has been from the East.

Indeed, the Arts have always turned to the East—to that Past which contains accomplishment and preserves tradition. To us here in the vast middle spaces of a great continent that eastern horizon is immediately the Atlantic seaboard, with its older civilization, its borrowed culture; it means New England and, latterly, New York. For upwards of a century in our national history the feet of youth, whenever stirred by art ambition, when eager for knowledge and training, have turned to the eastern seacoast, and though the stream has latterly not sought its first Mecca,—Boston and New England,—even today it persists in pouring into New York and on into Europe. But there are signs not hard to read that as a nation we are coming to the point when our young men of imagination and ideas will abandon this ancient pathway of the arts, or having obeyed the call, will return to their own soil, to the thing that has made them what they are, and seek imaginative satisfaction there. But I anticipate.

I was born and lived a good part of my life in that New England, within touch of the past, and, I am sorry to confess, with my face to the East. I can remember the hush that fell upon my town when Longfellow lay dead in his peaceful mansion facing the Charles, and I can recall the feeling that, with his death, American poetry had died. Now we see that Longfellow, like his fellow artists, like Copley and Bulfinch and Lowell, was scarcely American at all. For that puritan culture in which I was nurtured was but an imitation, an adaptation from an older civilization—a fine and delicate adaptation. We can see it today in the quiet streets of the seacoast towns, in Portland, Portsmouth, Salem—still fragrant with an atmosphere of other lands. Even in my day the reward of talent lay not in recognition at home, but abroad, in London and Paris. New England was ever protestant, and what it did not protest at in America at large, it ignored. I am afraid that it has not yet been cured of this mental squint. Nevertheless, imitative as was her art, her culture, it was far-reaching and noble. Long after Boston ceased to finance the west, she financed the country, so to speak, intellectually and morally, and when that large and impartial historian of our people comes to write the final record, he will give ample space to the barren and aristocratic province of New England.

The leadership in all matters has been passing from Boston, silently, surely, for a quarter-century—where? First to New York. Art and Letters follow trade, as always, and New York, that Colossus of Money, has absorbed into itself an undue portion of the literary and artistic culture of the nation, just as it has absorbed its money and its splendor. New York, itself of mixed tradition, has stolen, like a magnificent brigand. With its face eastwards, its many-fingered hands stretched out across the seas, it ransacks the earth, not in the New England spirit of imitation and adaptation, but in the spirit of material conquest. A few days ago I walked in company with a friend who was a stranger to the city, up and down the island, from the Battery and the canons about Wall street to where Grant's tomb is perched above the Hudson. Never before was the spectacle of our Titan so impressive to me. The predatory giant of America! Rebuilt, practically, within the last dozen years, on a colossal scale, with an unparalleled magnificence, New York is and will forever remain the Great Barbarian, the creature of spoil and pelf, rather than the Creator. From its gigantic campanile on Madison Square to its fortresses at the lower end of the island, it is a borrower, a parasite. Force, strength, splendor—these are New York's, but it has no life of its own. And it is the veriest commonplace to say that New York is anything but American.

Yet it is not strange that into this marvelous phenomenon of a city are pouring the artists and creators of our time. Here the imagination is stirred, here the rewards of fame are large and evident. Where are your painters and writers? I asked the men I met on the Pacific coast this summer. "Oh, gone to New York," was the almost universal reply. And elsewhere the story is the same, "Gone to New York!" In the belief that there are the buyers of pictures, the editors, the publishers, the play producers—there is the market for the artist's wares. And under the delusion that he must be near the market, at the counter, too often has a promising worker been sucked into the maelstrom, "where no man thinks, and the cry of the day is forgotten on the morrow." That this has been the tendency of our time, this fleeing to New York, this sucking into the great whirlpool, is too evident to be dwelt upon. The result? If America has no great art today, no distinctive expression, the blame is to be laid more than elsewhere at the door of New York. "I wish that the writers would keep out of New York," a great publisher said to me. "Why do the play writers persist in giving us pictures of New York society life?" the critics complain. Even New York is beginning to suspect, in moments of enlightenment and imagination, that it is not America!

I can remember when first I was in California, over twenty years ago, the surprise I had to find that books were published out there beyond the Rockies, that in this far-off land men painted pictures and wrote verse and built buildings. In short, that outside the great centers I had known, men lived and sought to express themselves, not merely performed the business of life. Since that early visit it has been my good fortune to return to the Western Coast twice, and to have touched many other parts of our country, and thus I have learned slowly what may be obvious to all of you, that our country differs from every other nation in the fact that here we have many centers of national vitality instead of one great cosmopolis. There are many points of radiancy, each with something of its own, and all with something common—something American. That people live and struggle, fight the fight, that they create about them a life with its own significance in many spots from the Atlantic to the Pacific—that is a great human fact. And where men organize their lives and create communities that are part of them—where they get children and make their homes, there they must find expression—in other words, art. And what we are to see in America I venture to say, is art springing up in many centers, not merely as one cosmopolitan head—everywhere where vital life goes forward. The day of local color, so called, has passed, thank God! and the day of community effort is beginning.

Really creative ideas are in the blood of the artist, are that part of him which is his not by will nor training, but by descent and inheritance. No matter how far he may roam, how he may transform himself into a cosmopolite, the real thing that he has to express will be what he draws from the soil where he was born, the conditions under which he and his parents lived. If this be true, and if it be true that all over our country there are centers of vital life demanding expression, we have that union of forces which must make for a national art that will be individual and strong.

New England had one supreme theme for expression: Man's adjustment with himself, his making of his peace with his God. New York has never had a theme of its own, anything fundamental demanding expression. But, latterly, voices have been heard from all parts of our great land that seem to carry the same message, that are efforts to phrase a mighty new theme. And that theme is, I believe, Man's adjustment with his fellowmen—the biggest and strongest theme that art has ever had to deal with. In the years immediately coming we shall hear this theme again and again expressed in multitudinous forms from many centers in our land.

He must be blind or completely ignorant of his times, who is not aware that already a new era of national ideals is upon us. As a nation we are not content with material accomplishment and mere efficiency, and discontent with a national life that holds but these two rewards must grow. We are seeking, as a people, for other human satisfactions, and surely one of these will be expression in art. Therefore I see before us the theme, the impulse, and the need.

I leave it to others, better qualified to speak than I, to phrase the opportunity that this new club of fellowship for the arts has before it. I take it, that our meeting tonight, that the opening of this club has very real significance for the community of Chicago. It means that those of us who are engaged in the practice of the arts, who are interested in the expression of our national life in something other than material accomplishment and mere efficiency, are to have a home, a gathering place where, in true fellowship, with sympathy and understanding and mutual helpfulness, we may meet together, and help create that life of the arts which will make future creation of real worth and significance more possible, if not for ourselves, for those others who are to come after and take up our work.

## OUR PRESENT.
ADDRESS BY CHARLES L. HUTCHINSON.

GENTLEMEN:—

YOUR kind reception has quite overwhelmed me and has put out of my mind the eloquent words I intended to speak. I am one of your honored Directors, and first, would say a word for them. You can imagine how busy and anxious they have been during the past few days in making the final preparations for the opening tonight. They are like the man who did business in Boston and lived at Worcester, making daily a trip between the two places. One day a severe snow storm prevented him from reaching Worcester, and the next morning he sent this telegram to his partner in Boston:

"Shall not be in town today, have not got home yesterday yet."

The Directors have no apology to offer. From what you see about us, you will appreciate what they have done and also what you may expect to find here when the work is completed.

I also wish to congratulate Mr. Howard Shaw, who has designed the interior of the room, and given much time to its construction. I can imagine how he felt as he watched the impressive ceremonies of the lighting of the fires upon our hearth, and wondered whether or not his chimney would smoke. It is not every architect who can build a chimney that will draw. How greatly relieved he must have been as he saw the flames roll up our chimney without interruption.

The Czar, Hamlin the First, has decreed that we shall consider tonight the past, the present and the future. With the past he associates literature, with the future, art, and with the present, commerce. So he has commanded a writer to speak of the past, an artist—I suppose a sculptor may be considered an artist—of the future, and me, an ordinary layman with a love for the artistic, to speak of the present. He first asked me to do this two days before Christmas, in the presence of the sculptor, whose mind was so full of the spirit of the season, and possibly of his needs at this time of great temptation, that he immediately thought of the present as a gift, instead of a period of time, and he said aloud that he thought it would be most appropriate for a layman, especially a banker, to present the present.

Who shall say that the artist is always impractical? There was wisdom in the speech of the sculptor. The Club is indebted to many of its members for valuable gifts, and could there be a more appropriate time to publicly acknowledge them than the present one?

Much of the furniture about us has been presented to the Club by some of its members. Among these are Mr. Glessner, Mr. Shaw, Mr. Gates, Mr. Ryerson, Mr. Chatfield-Taylor, Mr. Butler, Mr. Morris, Mr. Porter, and your humble servant.

As I thank these gentlemen on behalf of the Club for their generosity to it, our mercenary President suggests that I tell you there is still an opportunity for any member present to add his name to this distinguished list. The hint was taken by Mr. Bissell, Mr. Taft, Mr. C. F. Browne, Mr. Barnhart, Mr. Theo. Shaw, and Mr. Bartlett.

It seems that I am not to be allowed to appear before you, even upon this occasion, without a subscription paper in my hand. The suggestion of the President is an unfair one. I know my reputation in such matters is an evil one. President Angell of the Michigan University once said that should he survive me, he would preach my funeral sermon, and that his text was already chosen.

It was taken from the parable of the rich man and Lazarus, "And at last the beggar died also."

I wonder why "the Czar" made the particular combinations I have mentioned. Does he truly think that literature is dead, and that art has not yet arrived, and that for the time being, the ordinary, stupid, illiterate and inartistic layman occupies the stage? He may be right. He also suggested—and a suggestion from the Czar is a command—that I should speak of the benefits of the Club to the layman. Did he not think that the layman might be of benefit to the Club; did he forget that if it were not for the unintelligent layman that most of the literature produced to-day would not be read? Did he lose sight of the fact that it is the "would-be artistic" layman who buys most of the so-called works of art produced at the present time; who delights in purchasing spurious paintings when signed by forged names of Corot, Inness, and other popular masters? Who could ever rave over most of the music written at the present time, but an uncultivated layman? Indeed, I think a stupid layman is a handy thing to have about the house. He plays an important part in the lives of those who belong to the artistic world. It is true that there should not be too many of them in evidence, not more, say, than one in three—but how can we prevent their creation? We cannot keep them down.

Let us paint them out, that the canvas of the future may become truly artistic and harmonious. Still, harmony does not always exist among artists. Many singers have become notorious by their lack of harmony. I know a lot about laymen. It would not be wise to tell it all here; you might put some of us out and we wish to stay; not, however, as the Czar has said, for what we can get out of the Club, but rather for what we hope to bring to it. The mere mention of the word Czar suggests revolution, and that, I suppose, is why I wish to look upon the subject assigned to me by Hamlin the First, from exactly the opposite standpoint from which he offered it.

It is not well to ask how the Club can benefit the layman; it were better to put the question in this form: How can I, a layman, benefit the Club? If the life of the Club is to be one of interest and one in which all shall find pleasure and profit, every member of the Club must bring to it as much of goodfellowship as lies within him, and do his part cheerfully in creating interest and the proper atmosphere, so to speak. Therefore, it is my duty to do as the Czar commands. The Present is rather a large subject, and I hesitate to discuss it in an after-dinner speech. In doing so, however, I bear in mind the little girl who was told that she was to swim in the Atlantic Ocean, and said, "Well, I don't have to swim in all of it."

Let us rejoice that we live in the present age. The world has never seen a better one. There are many prophets among us who will not admit this. Denunciation of the present is their greatest pleasure. Do not take them too seriously. Such men have existed in every age. To them the Golden Age is ever behind us. To their fathers the age was worse than that of their grandfathers. They cried out against the present, like Jeremiah of old. No doubt just such lamentation was raised in the best ages of antiquity. Probably the son of him, who led by Moses, walked through the Red Sea—as well as the man whose father fought at Marathon, bewailed the degeneracy of the time in which he lived. Certainly we shun the society of some such prophets now. Are there not times when we ourselves join their numbers?

Sometimes with apparent reason we become discouraged. Like the poor man of New England who was about to die.

Just before he did so, he had a short period of consciousness, and said to his wife, "Maria, don't I smell ham cooking?" "Yes, John," she replied, "we are cooking a ham." "Well, give me a piece," he says. "It smells so good it would taste fine." "No, John," she replied, "you can't have any, it's for the mourners."

His greatest desire was at hand, but he was not allowed to partake of the feast, although it was to be spread in honor of himself.

Czar Hamlin was right when he assigned the present to the layman, for we live in the age of business. The dominant spirit of the time is commercial. Still, we need not despise this present or the conditions that surround the artistic world. This age of steel and machinery, of steam and electricity, with all its commercialism, is far better than the time when Imperial Rome dominated the world, far better than the Golden Age of Athens. Tyre and Sidon were once famous as the home of the Arts—these cities were built by Phoenician traders. Greek liberty and Greek literature sprang from the commercial spirit of the time. Little Holland was a country of merchants when she rescued from the almost universal ruin of the Middle Ages all that was best of the culture of the times.

If you will study the history of commerce, you will learn that it has been closely related to all the great movements for the uplifting of humanity. It is today one of the greatest agencies for the advancement of true civilization—which, after all, is only a knowledge of how to live and a will to use that knowledge. We have no need to be despondent, even here in smoky, commercial Chicago. There is more truth and righteousness in the world today than ever before. There is more of charity and harmony in the present than in the past. When in the history of mankind has a great disaster like that which has so recently overwhelmed the people of Italy, ever called forth such a universal response of sympathy and treasure? The moral integrity of God's universe is still intact. Literature and Art may go hand in hand with Commerce to advance the civilization of the world.

If we fail to find the good, the true and the beautiful in the present, is it not because we ourselves are growing old and narrow and sour? Do we not need to rise above our environment of self and realize how much the present has to offer? Here let me present a thought taken from an article in an English paper given me by a member of the Club. We all at times play the role of prophet, and it is well to do so, but do not take the part of one who cries:

"Return, oh, my people, return!" Rather be one to cry, "Go forward like men!"

Why do you look for a new Heaven and a new Earth in vanished things and outworn uses when all the time those Kingdoms are within you and their glory is still to be revealed? Let us come to the Club in such a spirit; bring to it the best of all that lies within us, of experience, of culture, of good fellowship and good cheer, and we will soon make of this place a shrine, not only of pleasure, but of inspiration. The more we give the more we shall receive.

Let us embrace the wealth of opportunity offered by the present, and rejoice in it and, perchance, in the future some prophet will arise and bemoan the fact that we and the glories of our present have passed away. Let us ask not what can the Club do for us, but what can I do for it.

Long live Czar Hamlin, the First, Founder of the Cliff Dwellers!

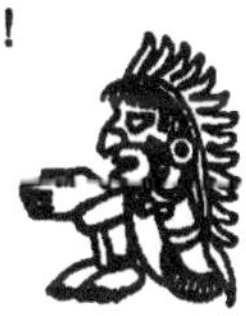

## SOME PERSONAL LETTERS.

THE NATIONAL INSTITUTE OF ARTS AND LETTERS, New York City.

"The National Institute of Arts and Letters, founded to promote co-operation and social intercourse among artists, musicians and men of letters, has special pleasure in sending fraternal greetings to The Cliff Dwellers, and in wishing it prosperity and good fellowship on its Parnassian heights.

"(Signed) W. M. SLOAN,
         "President."
    JOHN W. ALEXANDER,
    HAMILTON W. MABIE,
    ARTHUR WHITING,
    HAMLIN GARLAND,
       Vice-Presidents.
  ROBERT UNDERWOOD JOHNSON,
         Secretary.

From Richard Watson Gilder, of The Century Association, New York.

"To The Cliff Dwellers: As chairman of the Committee of Literature of The Century Association, I am by this committee, and by the secretary of the association, authorized to extend to The Cliff Dwellers most hearty fraternal greetings from the association in New York, which was so long ago established with like spirit and intent. From the height of our own long and happy history, we wish you a fortunate beginning and an everlasting continuing on your dwelling in the cliffs.

"My duty becomes all the more pleasing since I have just been informed by one Hamlin Garland that you have generously extended to me the much-anticipated advantages and opportunities of honorary membership, for which my best acknowledgment. With good hopes and prophecies, I am, "Very respectfully yours,
"Richard Watson Gilder."

From Edward Everett Hale, Washington, D. C.

"I am very glad that you have invited me to the meeting of Jan. 6th. It is a great pity that I cannot be there. You always have such a good time when you get together the bright particular lights at Chicago.

Will the new club have any library? Some time, I want to send something for it. My phrase above, "Have a good time," has been challenged, as being provincial in New England, but good John Dryden says, "The sons of Belial had a glorious time"; and we ought to be able to improve two or three centuries on him.

"Always truly yours,
"Edward E. Hale."

From JAMES LANE ALLEN, of Kentucky.

"You expressed in your recent letter to me a wish that I, a man of the South, should send to you, as president of The Cliff Dwellers' Club, of Chicago, a greeting to its members on the occasion, I believe, of the formal opening of the club. I am glad to do so, but the request brings up so many thoughts that I hesitate, in view of the fitting verity, as to my choice of the fittest theme.

"I think I shall begin by directing your attention to a social fact of immense significance, that the old South was a clubless land, and that the new South is an almost clubless land today—as respects men's clubs to be put to the service of the fine arts. As one consequence, nearly every best writer that the old South had, worked well nigh as a hermit or a wreck, and nearly every best writer of the new South has left it—to live elsewhere. Joel Chandler Harris was the solitary exception, and there were especial reasons of temperament for keeping him all his life at his home. The presence in the civilization of the South—old and new—of clubs for men, devoted to the work of fostering the fine arts would, I believe, have profoundly affected this part of its history.

"In the North, the formation of men's clubs has reached a stage of perfection, as reflects their mere structure. In the whole world, there are none that represent a higher development of what may be called organized convenience—organized comfort—organized learning—organized prestige. But I doubt whether the best clubs in our country —North or elsewhere—have as yet even dreamed of what they could do—and some day may do— for our civilization by becoming organized friendships or organized work. It has been said that clubs fought and won the French Revolution; that it is its clubs that are pushing France onward today; that it is clubs that are modernizing the Orient. Think how instantaneous the effect would be—what a thrill and an awakening it would send throughout our civilization, if tomorrow it were announced that the most powerful clubs in our country had begun a concerted movement to put the fine arts where they have never been, but where they have always belonged —at the very summit of our country's duty and truth and greatness.

"Perhaps your club may begin such a movement. I hope it may! and God bless us, everyone!         JAMES LANE ALLEN."

FROM THOS. NELSON PAGE.

"I assure you of my high appreciation of the honor done me by the invitation of The Cliff Dwellers to become a non-resident honorary member, so graciously conveyed by you, and of the great pleasure it gives me to accept the invitation. It is one of the clubs of which I have heard much, and only pleasant things, and I have long hoped to have the pleasure of meeting there the men who have done so much to place the stamp of originality on American letters and art. Some day I shall come knocking at your door and ask to be let in as an admirer of both the president and his constituents, and maybe, as one who claims that literature has no longitude, and wants to climb up to the perch where wit has its home, however far below he may scuffle in the dust.            "Faithfully yours,
"THOMAS NELSON PAGE."

From Col. Thos. Wentworth Higginson, Cambridge, Mass.

"Thank you for telling me about the new club you have organized in Chicago. My own associations with that city have been so agreeable, ever since the great exposition, when I was the guest of a most agreeable household; and also in connection with some later hospitalities, that I found it quite intelligible when I read that my dear old playmate, Norton, the most fastidious of men, had expressed willingness to spend his life there, were he to live it over again.

"On the other hand, I remember well that I once dined there with Howells, at some hospitable club, and had to leave it prematurely to catch a train; I remember how dear Eugene Field escorted me to the train, and when I begged him to go hastily back and finish his dinner, he answered me that I was saving him from dyspepsia for that one day, and that he always caught at any opportunity for retreating. But I remember that, although we did the best we could to keep Roswell Field here, and he still remains a member of our authors' club, he never looks in upon us, though we would gladly welcome him, and you, too, if you would come with (or even without) him. I should feel honored by being an honorary member, as you kindly suggest; but I am within three days of 85, and doubt if I ever see Chicago again.

"Cordially yours,
"Thomas Wentworth Higginson."

FROM W. D. HOWELLS, 10 W. 30th St., New York City.

"I have tried hard, but tried in vain, to write something fit to be read before The Cliff Dwellers on their opening night. I am comforted a little for any failure by the fact, which I have often noted, that nobody listens on such occasions, to the fittest words of the absent, and I console myself, therefore, the more easily in addressing to your private ear and eye my thanks for the honor your club has done me in choosing me a silent member, and my belief, hope and joy in its great future. You know already the high regard in which I hold the literary group of Chicago, beginning with Fuller, and including Herrick, Payne, Ade, Edith Wyatt, yourself, and, no doubt, others whose names will not occur to my aging memory. For nature and art and the union of both, I cannot think of any local group surpassing it, and if you extend your Chicago so as to take in Riley at Indianapolis, and Cawein at Louisville, and Whitlock at Toledo, where else shall the world match you? I suppose my western heart warms to you because you are westerners, and my sectional pride is touched, but I believe I love you and honor you most because you seem to be doing true and honest work in the right way.

"Yours affectionately,
"W. D. HOWELLS."

FROM S. WEIR MITCHELL, Philadelphia.

"As the president and founder of The Franklin Inn Club here, which represents with us that which The Tavern Club does in Boston, I send to your Cliff Dwellers a word of congratulation from civilization to our unfortunate brothers living in caves. "Yours truly,
"WEIR MITCHELL."

FROM DUFFIELD OSBORNE, Sec'y The Authors' Club, New York City.

"I regret that no meeting of our executive council will be held before January 6th. Personally, and in so far as a secretary may do on his own authority, let me tender you the sympathy with your purpose, and the good wishes for the success of your organization which, I am sure, the members of The Authors' Club will feel.
"Sincerely yours,
"DUFFIELD OSBORNE."

FROM JAMES WHITCOMB RILEY.

"It is with great delight that I just hear of your prospective housewarming of The Cliff Dwellers' Club. Even though an invalid, and of proportionately low spirits—I am still warmed and enthused over hearing of your new organization. All hail! Fraternal greetings to your members, one and all.
"As ever and always, yours,
"JAMES WHITCOMB RILEY."

# OFFICERS, BOARD OF DIRECTORS AND COMMITTEES.

## OFFICERS AND BOARD OF DIRECTORS FOR 1910.

HAMLIN GARLAND, President
FREDERICK ROOT, Vice-President
FRANK G. LOGAN, Treasurer
ARTHUR T. ALDIS, Secretary

RALPH CLARKSON     DONALD ROBERTSON
CHARLES L. HUTCHINSON     LORADO TAFT
HOWARD SHAW

## OFFICERS AND BOARD OF DIRECTORS FOR 1908 AND 1909.

HAMLIN GARLAND, President
HOWARD SHAW, Vice-President
RALPH CLARKSON, Secretary
CHARLES L. HUTCHINSON, Treasurer

FRANK G. LOGAN     ARTHUR ALDIS
DONALD ROBERTSON     CLARENCE DICKINSON
LORADO TAFT

## COMMITTEES FOR 1910.

### ART COMMITTEE

RALPH CLARKSON      FREDERICK C. BARTLETT
WILSON IRVINE

### HOUSE COMMITTEE

N. H. CARPENTER      RALPH FLETCHER SEYMOUR
HOBART CHATFIELD-TAYLOR

### ENTERTAINMENT COMMITTEE

THOMAS WOOD STEVENS    ARTHUR HUEN
ARTHUR OLAF ANDERSON    BERT L. TAYLOR
RALPH HOLMES            JOHN CARPENTER
KARL E. HARRIMAN

### RECEPTION COMMITTEE

HOBART CHATFIELD-TAYLOR   HARRY PRATT JUDSON
ABRAM W. HARRIS          WM. M. R. FRENCH
GLENN D. GUNN            IRA NELSON MORRIS
KARL E. HARRIMAN        ROSWELL FIELD
KARLTON HACKETT

### LIBRARIAN

WALLACE RICE.

### ART COMMITTEE
Lorado Taft  Frederick C. Bartlett
Ralph Clarkson

### HOUSE COMMITTEE
Arthur T. Aldis  Ralph Fletcher Seymour
Ralph Poole

### LIBRARIAN
Frederick Ives Carpenter

### AUDITING COMMITTEE
Charles R. Crane  C. C. Curtiss
John T. McCutcheon

### BUILDING COMMITTEE
Charles L. Hutchinson  Howard Shaw
I. K. Pond

# CONSTITUTION
## OF THE
# CLIFF-DWELLERS

*Committee on Constitution*
JOHN T. MCCUTCHEON, *Chairman*
LORADO TAFT             WALLACE RICE

ADOPTED
VI NOVEMBER
MCMVII

# CONSTITUTION

## ARTICLE I.
### NAME.

The name of this Club is The Cliff-Dwellers.

## ARTICLE II.
### OFFICERS.

The officers of the Club shall be a President, a Vice-President, a Secretary, and a Treasurer, who shall be elected annually by the Board of Directors from its own body, and shall hold office until their successors are elected.

## ARTICLE III.
### PRESIDENT.

The President, or in his absence the Vice-President, shall preside at the meetings of the Club and of the Board of Directors. In the absence of both officers, a meeting of the Club or of the Board of Directors shall elect its presiding officer. The President shall, with the

Secretary, sign all written contracts and obligations of the Club, and shall perform such other duties as the Board of Directors may assign him.

## ARTICLE IV.
### TREASURER.

The Treasurer shall collect all entrance fees and other dues, shall keep the accounts of the Club, and shall report thereon at each regular meeting of the Board of Directors. His accounts shall be annually audited by the Auditing Committee. He shall pay all bills on the certificate of their correctness by the House Committee or the Art Committee. He shall keep all funds of the Club in the bank or place of deposit named by the Board of Directors. He shall notify successful candidates of their election to membership.

## ARTICLE V.
### SECRETARY.

The Secretary shall give notice of all meetings of the Club and of the Board of Directors, and shall keep minutes of such meetings. He shall conduct the correspondence, and keep the records of the Club. He shall notify to the

Treasurer the names of all persons elected to membership, and shall be the keeper of the seal of the Club.

## ARTICLE VI.
### DIRECTORS.

Section 1. The government and management of the Club shall repose in a Board of nine Directors, to be elected at the annual meeting of the Club.

Sec. 2. The Board of Directors shall control the affairs of the Club, provide for its government, elect its members, take cognizance of all infractions of its constitution and by-laws, and fill vacancies in its own body until the next regular election.

Sec. 3. They shall all be resident members, and at least six of them shall be professionally concerned with The Fine Arts.

Sec. 4. The Board of Directors shall meet once a month. Special meetings may be called by order of the President or of the House Committee. Five Directors shall constitute a quorum of the Board.

Sec. 5. The Board of Directors first elected shall by lot divide its members into three classes of three each, the term of office of the first of which shall expire in 1909, of the second in 1910, and of the third in 1911, and their successors thereafter shall be elected at the annual meeting of the Club, together with the successors to any vacancies arising during the year and temporarily filled by the Board of Directors. Thereafter all Directors shall hold office for the term of three years, and until their successors are chosen and have accepted office.

Sec. 6. A two-thirds vote of the resident members voting shall be necessary to elect to the Board of Directors.

## ARTICLE VII.
### MEETINGS.

Section 1. The annual meeting of the Club shall be held on the first Monday after Twelfth-night (January *sixth*) in each year, at which meeting the Board of Directors shall render to the members a report of the affairs of the Club during the twelve-month preceding.

Sec. 2. Upon the written request of twenty-five members the Board of Directors shall call a meeting of the Club, which request, and also the notice of any such special meetings, shall state the object for which such meeting is called; and at a special meeting no object not so stated shall be considered.

Sec. 3. Notices of all meetings, annual and special, shall be posted in the rooms of the Club for one week. One-fifth of the resident membership shall constitute a quorum.

## ARTICLE VIII.
### MEMBERS.

Section 1. Any male person of twenty-five years or more shall be eligible to professional membership who is professionally engaged in literature, painting, sculpture, architecture, music, or the drama, or to lay membership who is a connoisseur and lover of The Fine Arts.

Sec. 2. Every candidate for membership shall be twenty-five years of age when proposed, and shall be proposed and seconded by two members of the Club, neither of whom may be members of the Board of Directors. The name, occupation, and residence of the candidate, and the names of his proposer and seconder in their own handwriting, shall be placed in a book kept for that purpose at least fourteen days before balloting; the names of the candidate and of his proposer and seconder shall be posted on the bulletin board of the Club at least fourteen days before the day of election.

Sec. 3. Balloting for members shall take place at stated meetings only of the Board of Directors.

Sec. 4. Five affirmative votes are necessary to elect any candidate, and two black balls shall exclude.

Sec. 5. All proceedings of the Board regarding elections shall be kept by each member in strict secrecy.

Sec. 6. The House Committee may in its discretion admit by invitation distinguished strangers as visitors of the Club.

Sec. 7. The number of resident members of the Club shall not exceed two hundred and fifty, of whom never more than one hundred shall be lay members; and the number of non-resident members shall be as fixed by the Board of Directors from time to time.

Sec. 8. Resignations of membership shall be made to the Secretary in writing, and accepted by the Board of Directors. The resingation of any member who is in arrears for dues shall not be accepted.

## ARTICLE IX.
### DUES.

Section 1. The entrance fee shall be fifty dollars for resident members; and each non-resident member, elected as such, who shall become a resident member, shall pay fifty dollars to the Treasurer; and a failure to pay such sum shall be considered a failure to pay dues.

Sec. 2. The annual dues of resident members shall be forty dollars, payable quarterly in advance on the first days of January, April, July, and October; and of non-resident members fifteen dollars, payable annually in advance.

Sec. 3. Persons not residing or having places of business in the city of Chicago or its suburbs may be elected as non-resident members. Any resident member who removes his residence and place of business from the city of Chicago and its suburbs, on written notice to the Treasurer of such removal, may become a non-resident member; and should a resident member so removed and become a non-resident member wish to become a resident member again he shall not be required to pay any additional entrance fee, upon notifying the Treasurer of such return.

Sec. 4. Candidates elected, on payment of the entrance fee and of the dues for the first quarter, or in the case of non-resident members, of the annual dues only, shall become members of the Club. The election of any candidate shall be void if he fail to make such payment within thirty days after notice of his election is mailed to him at the address given by his proposer and seconder.

Sec. 5. When the dues of any member shall remain unpaid for the space of three months, the Treasurer shall cause him to be notified that, unless the dues in arrears are paid within thirty days thereafter, his membership shall cease; and in case such dues are not paid pursuant to such notice, or such default is not accounted for to the satisfaction of the Board of Directors, he shall thereupon cease to be a member.

Sec. 6. The Board of Directors, by unanimous vote of those present at any stated meeting, is empowered to remit, wholly or in part, the entrance fee or dues of any member.

## ARTICLE X.
### EXPULSION AND SUSPENSION.

Any member may be suspended or expelled for cause by a vote of two-thirds of all the members of the Board of Directors, one month's previous notice in writing having been duly mailed to such member's address, with a copy of the charge preferred against him.

## ARTICLE XI.
### GAMBLING.

No betting, dicing, or card-playing shall be allowed in the Club.

## ARTICLE XII.
### RULES.

The Board of Directors shall prepare and enforce rules regulating the use of the Club rooms by the members.

## ARTICLE XIII.
### HOUSE COMMITTEE.

The Board of Directors shall annually appoint from its own members, or from the membership of the Club, or both, a House Committee of three persons, which shall have charge of the Club rooms, subject to the control of the Board of Directors, shall hire and discharge all employees, shall receive all complaints of members and report upon the same to the Board of Directors, shall procure necessary articles for the use and convenience of the members, and shall render to the Board of Directors a monthly report of all supplies bought and sold during the previous month, and on hand at its close.

## ARTICLE XIV.
### AUDITING COMMITTEE.

The Board of Directors shall annually appoint from its own members, or from the membership of the Club, or both, an Auditing Committee of three persons, which shall audit the accounts of the Treasurer annually, and report to the Board the accounts audited and allowed.

## ARTICLE XV.
### ART COMMITTEE.

The Board of Directors shall annually appoint from its own members, or from the membership of the Club, or both, an Art Committee of three persons, which, subject to the control of the Board of Directors, shall have charge of the books, papers, and works of art of the Club; shall have power to solicit and receive gifts, and to select and purchase books, periodicals, and works of art for the Club; shall render to the Board of Directors a monthly report of all gifts and purchases; and shall annually recommend for appointment by the Board of Directors a Librarian.

## ARTICLE XVI.
### LIBRARIAN.

The Librarian shall be a member of the Club, and shall have custody of all books, drawings, musical compositions, photographs, and other works of art of the Club, and shall establish and maintain a catalogue of the same.

## ARTICLE XVII.
### NOTICES.

Each member shall enter in a book kept for that purpose a mail address, to which all notices to be sent to him under the Constitution or rules shall be directed. In default of such entry, such notices shall be served by depositing them in the Club letter box, addressed to the member, who shall be held to have received them ten days after they shall have been so mailed or deposited.

## ARTICLE XVIII.
### AMENDMENTS.

This Constitution may be amended at any annual meeting of the Club, or at a special meeting of the Club, or at a special meeting called for that purpose, by a two-thirds vote of the resident members present and voting, providing the proposed amendment shall have been subscribed by at least ten members of the Club in residence, and shall have been duly presented to the President of the Club, and shall have been posted upon the bulletin board of the Club at least fourteen days before such meeting. A notice of the proposed amendment shall be mailed to every resident member at least ten days before the meeting of the Club at which such amendment is to be considered.

## ARTICLE XIX.
### FINAL APPEAL.

The interpretation of this Constitution and of all rules empowered by it shall rest with the Board of Directors.

## LIST OF MEMBERS.

Single stars signify non-resident members.

| | |
|---|---|
| GEORGE ADE | Brook, Indiana |
| ARTHUR T. ALDIS | 247 Monadnock Building |
| OWEN FRANKLIN ALDIS | 247 Monadnock Building |
| *ROBERT ALLERTON | Monticello, Ill. |
| ARTHUR OLAF ANDERSON | Fine Arts Building |
| PIERCE ANDERSON | Railway Exchange Building |
| CLEMENT W. ANDREWS | 87 Wabash Avenue |
| EDWARD E. AYER | 1515 Railway Exchange Building |
| JAMES R. ANGELL | 5551 Lexington Avenue |
| JOHN K. ALLEN | 209 N. Jefferson Street |
| CHARLES THOMPSON ATKINSON | Chicago Stock Exchange |
| ALFRED L. BAKER | 209 LaSalle Street |
| EDGAR A. BANCROFT | 237 Michigan Avenue |
| ARTHUR M. BARNHART | 185 Monroe Street |
| FRANK BARRY | 1505 Lincoln Street, Evanston |
| ADOLPHUS C. BARTLETT | 1 State Street |
| FREDERICK C. BARTLETT | 2901 Prairie Avenue |
| SOLON S. BEMAN | Harvester Building |
| E. H. BENNETT | 1800 Railway Exchange Building |
| *DAVID BISPHAM | 44 W. 44th St., New York City |
| ARTHUR BISSELL | Fine Arts Building |
| LOUIS J. BLOCK | 614 Washington Boulevard |
| PERCY H. BOYNTON | University of Chicago |
| JOHN DORR BRADLEY | Monadnock Block |
| ARTHUR C. L. BROWN | Northwestern University, Evanston |
| CHAS. FRANCIS BROWNE | 1543 East 57th Street |

*SCOTT BROWN ........................South Bend, Ind.
CLARENCE BUCKINGHAM................653 The Rookery
CLARENCE A. BURLEY.................122 Monroe Street
DANIEL H. BURNHAM..1417 Railway Exchange Building
ARTHUR M. BURTON.............618 Fine Arts Building
*RICHARD BURTON..State University, Minneapolis, Minn.
EDWARD B. BUTLER............7 West Randolph Street
HERBERT BUTLER...............712-243 Wabash Avenue
JAMES H. BREASTED............5533 Lexington Avenue
W. J. CALHOUN......................217 LaSalle Street
EDGAR S. CAMERON...................15 Studio Building
BENJAMIN CARPENTER.........208 South Water Street
FREDERICK I. CARPENTER........5533 Woodlawn Avenue
JOHN A. CARPENTER............208 South Water Street
NEWTON H. CARPENTER....................Art Institute
GEORGE WALLACE CARR...................Steinway Hall
*MADISON CAWEIN..18 St. James Court, Louisville, Ky.
HOBART C. CHATFIELD-TAYLOR..........631 Rush Street
RALPH CLARKSON..............1014 Fine Arts Building
DAVID A. CLIPPINGER..........410-243 Wabash Avenue
WALTER M. CLUTE........................Art Institute
S. H. CLARK......................University of Chicago
ROSSITER COLE...................721 Fine Arts Building
*ERNESTO CONSOLO................Lugano, Switzerland
HART CONWAY ....................243 Wabash Avenue
*HOLMES C. COWPER................Des Moines, Iowa
CHARLES R. CRANE..............2559 Michigan Avenue
LEONARD CRUNELLE...................Edison Park, Ill.
CHARLES C. CURTIS.............538 Fine Arts Building
*WALTER DAMROSCH..................New York City
HENRI DAVID....................5469 Madison Avenue
CHARLES G. DAWES.................152 Monroe Street
ARTHUR R. DEAN...................218 LaSalle Street

GEORGE R. DEAN......................218 LaSalle Street
J. SPENCER DICKERSON.........700 East Fortieth Street
*CLARENCE DICKINSON..................New York City
*JACOB M. DICKINSON..............Washington, D. C.
FREDERICK P. DINKELBERG............135 Adams Street
THOMAS E. DONNELLEY........Lakeside Press Building
GEORGE A. DORSEY................5637 Madison Avenue
FRANK V. DUDLEY..............East Sixty-third Street
ARTHUR DUNHAM........119 East Twenty-first Street
DAVID D. DUGGAN..................243 Wabash Avenue
PERCY B. ECKHART...........First Nat'l Bank Building
JAMES J. EGAN.................715-85 Dearborn Street
VICTOR ELTING........................706 The Rookery
*WALTER J. ENRIGHT.....................New York City
WILLIAM K. FELLOWS........1733-204 Dearborn Street
ROSWELL M. FIELD.....:.......4747 Magnolia Avenue
WALTER L. FISHER.............55-107 Dearborn Street
HORACE SPENCER FISKE..1373 East Fifty-seventh Street
WM. M. R. FRENCH..............Art Institute, Chicago
ISAAC K. FRIEDMAN......................Winnetka, Ill.
CHARLES S. FROST...............806-184 LaSalle Street
SHIRLEY M. K. GANDELL...........Auditorium Building
HAMLIN GARLAND..............6427 Greenwood Avenue
VICTOR GARWOOD..............614-243 Wabash Avenue
WM. D. GATES.............602-138 Washington Street
JOHN J. GLESSNER.................237 Michigan Avenue
KENNETH GOODMAN...........5026 Greenwood Avenue
WM. O. GOODMAN............5026 Greenwood Avenue
ALFRED HOYT GRANGER..........806-184 LaSalle Street
GEO. A. GRANT-SHAEFER............Fine Arts Building
MARION GREEN.....................Auditorium Building
GLENN DILLARD GUNN..........421 Fine Arts Building
*OLIVER D. GROVER.......................Florence, Italy

KARLETON HACKETT............5482 East End Avenue
JOHN L. HAMILTON...........1218-140 Dearborn Street
GEORGE HAMLIN...............5528 Woodlawn Avenue
ERNEST A. HAMILL............Corn Exch. Nat'l Bank
GUY HARDY.......................Fine Arts Building
KARL EDWIN HARRIMAN....Red Book, 158 State Street
H. B. HARVEY..................219 East Ohio Street
ABRAM WEINGARDNER HARRIS....N. W. University
                 Evanston
JAMES TAFT HATFIELD......617 Foster Street, Evanston
JOHN J. HATTSTAEDT..........614-243 Wabash Avenue
FRANKLIN H. HEAD....................3 Banks Street
WALLACE HECKMAN............1210-135 Adams Street
*HUGO HEERMAN......................Cincinnati, Ohio
HAROLD HENRY..................5510 Monroe Avenue
*MARK A. DEWOFE HOWE.........Tavern Club, Boston
*ROBERT HERRICK................University of Chicago
ARTHUR HEUN.....................810 Steinway Hall
FREDERICK C. HIBBARD.............652 East 60th Street
BURTON HOLMES.......................Congress Hotel
RALPH HOLMES.........................Art Institute
HENRY K. HOLSMAN..........444 Monadnock Building
CLARENCE A. HOUGH......617 West Jackson Boulevard
EMERSON HOUGH...............1808-115 Adams Street
W. L. HUBBARD......................Chicago Tribune
W. R. HUNT..........................Steinway Hall
CHARLES L. HUTCHINSON............217 LaSalle Street
HENRY M. HYDE............58th and Drexel Avenue
WILSON H. IRVINE.........1246 West Fifteenth Street
EDMUND J. JAMES....................Champaign, Ill.
ROBERT R. JARVIE........1340 East Forty-seventh Street
ELMER C. JENSEN..............1401-171 LaSalle Street
JENS JENSEN ...............604 N. Sacramento Avenue

JAMES R. JEWETT..............5757 Lexington Avenue
THOMAS D. JONES....................Lake Forest, Ill.
HARRY PRATT JUDSON......University of Chicago
                                     President's Office
ALFRED JUERGENS......203 S. Grove Avenue, Oak Park
JAMES HOWARD KEHLER..........203 Michigan Avenue
WALTER KELLER.................729 Fine Arts Building
WILLIAM KENT.....................12 Sherman Street
ALBERT H. KREHBIEL.......................Art Institute
WILMAT LAMONT...................Fine Arts Building
WALTER C. LARNED...........720-325 Dearborn Street
BRYAN LATHROP....................120 Bellevue Place
GARDNER LATHROP..........Railway Exchange Building
L. L. LAZELLE......................Fine Arts Building
HENIOT LEVY.................614, 243 Wabash Avenue
FRANK G. LOGAN.................2919 Prairie Avenue
THEODORE LOESCHER.......1417 Railway Exch. Building
*GEORGE HORACE LORIMER.....Saturday Evening Post,
                                     Philadelphia, Pa.
ROBERT M. LOVETT..................220 Sixtieth Street
P. C. LUTKIN......Northwestern University, Evanston
JULIAN W. MACK......................Ashland Block
FRANKLIN MACVEAGH.............29 Wabash Avenue
*I. F. MARCOSSON.........The Players, New York City
HUGH G. McBIRNEY..............1627 Prairie Avenue
CYRUS H. McCORMICK............237 Michigan Avenue
HAROLD McCORMICK.............237 Michigan Avenue
GEORGE BARR McCUTCHEON............66 Cedar Street
JOHN T. McCUTCHEON.........1018 Fine Arts Building
GEORGE H. MEAD............6016 Jackson Park Avenue
EVERETT L. MILLARD.......1110-100 Washington Street
RALPH MOJESKI.............1750 Monadnock Building
*WILLIAM VAUGHN MOODY.......University of Chicago

IRA N. MORRIS..................3401 Michigan Avenue
RICHARD G. MOULTON.........5053 Washington Avenue
CHARLES J. MULLIGAN......722 South Ridgeway Avenue
WILLIAM B. MUNDIE.........1401-171 LaSalle Street
GEORGE C. NIMMONS........1733-204 Dearborn Street
CHARLES E. NIXON...............256 Michigan Avenue
*JOHN W. NORTON...................Lockport, Illinois
HORACE OAKLEY....................1142 The Rookery
ARNE OLDBERG.......Northwestern University, Evanston
CURTIS HIDDEN PAGE.....Northwestern University,
                 Evanston
GEORGE PARKARD.............1050-164 Dearborn Street
A. K. PARKER..................University of Chicago
JAMES WILLIAM PATTISON................Art Institute
*WILL PAYNE .......................Paw Paw, Mich.
WILLIAM M. PAYNE................Fine Arts Building
GEORGE R. PECK...........Railway Exchange Building
ALLEN E. PHILBRICK.................The Art Institute
FRANK C. PEYRAUD..............6037 Jefferson Avenue
RALPH H. POOLE...........414-169 Jackson Boulevard
ALLEN B. POND....................1109 Steinway Hall
IRVING K. POND...................1109 Steinway Hall
GEORGE F. PORTER............1622-143 Dearborn Street
J. WELLINGTON REYNOLDS............19 Pearson Street
WALLACE RICE.................4820 Champlain Avenue
*FREDERICK RICHARDSON................New York City
W. B. S. RICHARDSON............5510 Monroe Avenue
GEORGE ROBARD......1417 Railway Exchange Building
DONALD ROBERTSON................Champlain Building
MARTIN ROCHE..................98 Jackson Boulevard
LEON ROECKER................481 Forty-second Place
JOHN A. ROGERS...................1615-59 Clark Street
FREDERIC W. ROOT.............715-243 Wabash Avenue

| | |
|---|---|
| Martin A. Ryerson | 1221, 206 La Salle Street |
| Rollin D. Salisbury | 5730 Woodlawn Avenue |
| *A. C. Schillinger | German Consulate |
| Richard E. Schmidt | 701-172 Washington Street |
| Edwin Schneider | Fine Arts Building |
| Frank H. Scott | 184 LaSalle Street |
| *Ernest Thompson-Seton | Cos Cob, Conn. |
| Ralph Fletcher Seymour | Fine Arts Building |
| Guido Sabetta | Masonic Temple |
| J. C. Shaffer | Evening Post |
| Howard Shaw | 172-161 State Street |
| Theodore A. Shaw | 256 Market Street |
| William H. Sherwood | 713 Fine Arts Building |
| Paul Shorey | 5516 Woodlawn Avenue |
| George Schultz | 1158 Perry Street |
| Joseph L. Silsbee | 813, 115 Dearborn Street |
| Ossian C. Simonds | 1431 Montrose Avenue |
| Frederick J. V. Skiff | Box No. 223, Kenilworth, Ill. |
| Harold C. Smith | 1210 Astor Street |
| Allen Spencer | 4409 Sidney Avenue |
| Robert C. Spencer | 1200, 17 Van Buren Street |
| Albert A. Sprague | 600 Erie Street |
| Walter Spry | Fine Arts Building |
| John F. Stacey | 21 Studio Building |
| Thomas W. Stevens | 5706 Jackson Park Avenue |
| *W. D. Stevens | The Players, New York City |
| Frederick A. Stock | 405, 168 Michigan Avenue |
| Herbert S. Stone | 1324, 209 State Street |
| Clayton F. Summy | 220 Wabash Avenue |
| John Sutcliffe | 624, 218 La Salle Street |
| *Gardner Symons | New York City |
| Sidney Richmond Taber | 532 Monadnock Block |
| Lorado Taft | 1038 Fine Arts Building |

Frank B. Tarbell...............University of Chicago
*Booth Tarkington.................Indianapolis, Ind.
Bert Leston Taylor............5526 Everett Avenue
James W. Thompson...........University of Chicago
Slason Thompson........1409 Railway Exch. Building
Samuel A. Treat............1507, 279 Dearborn Street
George E. Vincent.............5737 Lexington Avenue
Frederick C. Walton..............816 N. State Street
L. H. Watson........................100 State Street
Peter J. Weber...................2117 Fisher Building
J. Clarence Webster..............706, 100 State Street
Henry K. Webster.....1403 Maple Ave., Evanston, Ill.
Adolph Weidig....................243 Wabash Avenue
Frederick J. Wessels...........168 Michigan Avenue
Chas. E. White............615 Lake Street, Oak Park
*Will Allen White.....................Emporia, Kan.
*Brand Whitlock........................Toledo, Ohio
William Carver Williams.......Auditorium Building
Louis W. Wilson................1306, 209 State Street
James H. Winn..............818 Fine Arts Building
Francis A. Winslow.........2515 W. Harrison Street
William H. Winslow........2515 W. Harrison Street
Arthur F. Woltersdorf..........22, 70 La Salle Street
Ernest Woodyatt................1615, 59 Clark Street
Robert G. Work......................161 State Street
Joseph Zeisler................3256 Lake Park Avenue
Sigmund Zeisler............1037, 164 Dearborn Street
F. Ziegfeld, Sr.................Chicago Musical College
W. Carbys Zimmerman............1101 Steinway Hall
William E. Zeuch.............6006 Kenmore Avenue

DECEASED.
Julian Yale, 1908.

## HONORARY MEMBERS.

John W. Alexander.........116 East 65th Street,
 New York City
James Lane Allen....130 W. 57th St., New York City
J. W. Dickinson........War Office, Washington, D. C.
Alfred East.......................London, England
Daniel Chester French....125 W. 11th Street,
 New York City
Thomas Wentworth Higginson.....Cambridge, Mass.
Wm. Dean Howells...........130 W. 57th Street,
 New York City
Robert Underwood Johnson......33 Union Square,
 New York City
A. Lawrence Lowell.........Harvard University,
 Cambridge, Mass.
Chas. F. Lummis..................Los Angeles, Calif.
Edwin Markham.........New Brighton, Staten Island
Joaquin Miller........................Oakland, Cal.
S. Weir Mitchell............1524 Chestnut Street,
 Philadelphia
Alphonse Mucha.............................. Paris
Brander Matthews..............Columbia University
Horatio Parker..................Yale University,
 New Haven, Conn.
James Whitcomb Riley.............Indianapolis, Ind.
F. Hopkinson Smith...........150 E. 34th Street,
 New York City
Otis Skinner............The Players, New York City
Augustus Thomas........The Lambs, New York City

### DECEASED.

Richard Watson Gilder.........33 Union Square,
 New York City
Edward Everett Hale................Roxbury, Mass.

RALPH FLETCHER SEYMOUR COMPANY
THE ALDERBRINK PRESS

CPSIA information can be obtained
at www.ICGtesting.com
Printed in the USA
LVHW081512260722
724456LV00004B/53